eking religion

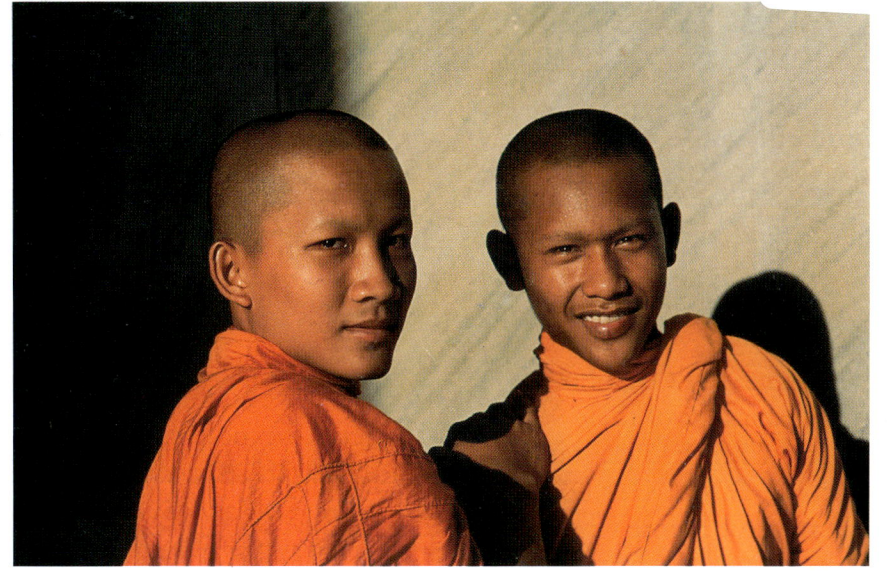

The **Buddhist** Experience

Jan Thompson

Foundation

Hodder & Stoughton
A MEMBER OF THE HODDER HEADLINE GROUP

Acknowledgements

Dedicated to:
Ann Lovelace, a friend and colleague.

Notes:

> CE = Common Era.
> BCE = Before the Common Era.
> CE corresponds to AD, and BCE corresponds to BC. The years are the same, but CE and BCE can be used by anyone regardless of their religion. (AD and BC are Christian: AD stands for Anno Domini – in the Year of Our Lord, i.e. Jesus Christ; BC stands for Before Christ.)

Key words are explained in the Glossary on page 63

The publishers would like to thank the following for permission to reproduce copyright material in this book:

Penguin Books Ltd for the extracts from *The Dhammapada*, translated by Juan Mascaro, 1973. Reproduced by permission; Denise Cush for the interview extract on page 54.

The publishers would like to thank the following for permission to reproduce copyright photographs in this book:
J Allan Cash: pp17, 25l, 51; Circa Photo Library: pp5tl, 9, 26r, 42, 43, 46t (William Holtby), 36; Corbis: pp5 centre (Mitchell Gerber), 32l (Sakamoto Photo Research Lab); Croydon Buddhist Centre: p5br; Phillip Emmett: pp11, 17 19, 41; The Hutchison Picture Library: pp25r, 44 (Patricio Goycoolea); Christine Osborne/MEP: pp13, 26l, 28, 29l, 46b, 47r (J Worker), 52b (N Dawson); Ann and Bury Peerless: pp6, 37; Popperfoto: p7; The Ronald Grant Archive: p58; David Rose: pp5tr, 22, 23, 27, 39r, 40, 47l, 52t, 54r; Tony Halls/Science Photo Library: p12; Kevin Shaw: 29r; Mel Thompson: pp4, 5bl, 16, 24r, 31, 32r, 38, 39l, 54l, 59, 62.

Minor adaptations have been made to some quotations to render them more accessible to the readership.

Every effort has been made to contact the holders of copyright material but if any have been inadvertently overlooked, the publisher will be pleased to make the necessary alterations at the first opportunity.

Orders: please contact Bookpoint Ltd, 130 Milton Park, Abingdon, Oxon OX14 4SB. Telephone: (44) 01235 827720, Fax: (44) 01235 400454. Lines are open from 9.00–6.00, Monday to Saturday, with a 24 hour message answering service. Email address: orders@bookpoint.co.uk

British Library Cataloguing in Publication Data
A catalogue record for this title is available from The British Library

ISBN 0 340 77583 1

| Impression number | 10 9 8 7 6 5 4 3 |
| Year | 2005 2004 2003 2002 2001 |

Copyright © 2000 Jan Thompson and Mel Thompson

All rights reserved. No part of this publication may be reproduced or transmitted in any form or by any means, electronic or mechanical, including photocopy, recording, or any information storage and retrieval system, without permission in writing from the publisher or under licence from the Copyright Licensing Agency Limited. Further details of such licences (for reprographic reproduction) may be obtained from the Copyright Licensing Agency Limited, of 90 Tottenham Court Road, London W1P 9HE.

All illustrations supplied by Daedalus, with special thanks to John McIntyre and Steve Parkhouse
Cover photo from CIRCA Photo Library
Typeset by Wearset, Boldon, Tyne and Wear.
Printed for Hodder & Stoughton Educational, a division of Hodder Headline Plc, 338 Euston Road, London NW1 3BH by Printer Trento, Italy

Contents

1	What is Buddhism?	*4*
2	A Man called Siddhartha	*6*
3	Siddhartha's Quest	*8*
4	The Enlightened One (Buddha)	*10*
5	The Buddha's Teaching (Dharma)	*12*
6	The Community (Sangha)	*18*
7	Different Kinds of Buddhism	*20*
8	Going for Refuge	*30*
9	Buddha Images	*32*
10	At a Shrine	*38*
11	Meditation	*42*
12	Festivals	*46*
13	The Buddhist Way of Life	*48*
14	Buddhist Scriptures	*52*
15	Women in Buddhism	*54*
16	The Wheel of Life	*56*
17	The Perfections	*60*
18	Living it out	*62*
	Glossary	*63*
	Index	*64*

1 What is Buddhism?

> **TASK**
> There is a lot of suffering in the world. Give some examples.

Buddhism is a way of life. It is based on the teachings of a man who lived in India about 2500 years ago. He was called the Buddha. Most Buddhists come from the Far East, but many Westerners are now interested in Buddhism.

● Questions about Buddhism

What is Buddhism about?
Buddhism wants people to be happy. It wants to stop suffering.

But how can we be happy? Some people think they will be happy if they win the lottery, or if they fall in love, or if they get a good job. But money is quickly spent, people fall out of love, and they can lose their jobs. For many people, life is never quite right. They are not really happy. There is always some kind of suffering.

Buddhism helps people to look quietly and carefully at life. It helps them to think about what actually makes them happy or unhappy.

Buddhists spend a lot of time thinking about themselves. They believe that you can't really understand and help other people until you understand yourself. But they do care about others, and about all living things.

Key words	
Buddhism	Buddha
Buddhist	meditate

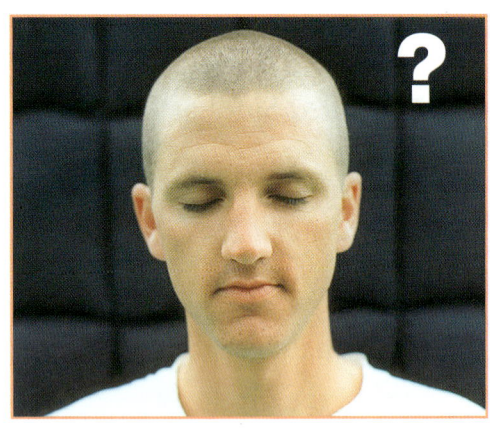

Is Buddhism a religion?
This might seem a strange question to ask, when you are studying Buddhism in RE. But there are things about Buddhism which are religious, and there are things about it which aren't.

Buddhism is like a religion in that:
* it has places of worship
* Buddhists offer gifts to Buddha images
* they meditate (this is a form of prayer)
* there are holy books
* Buddhists follow the teachings of a holy man
* Buddhism is a way of life.

Buddhism is unlike a religion in that:
* Buddhists are not told what to believe – they can form their own ideas.
* Buddhism doesn't say that there is a God, and it doesn't say that there isn't a God!
* a person can be a Buddhist without going to a place of worship and without doing religious things.

So there is no simple answer to the question 'Is Buddhism a religion?'

How can you spot a Buddhist?
Well, take a look at the photos on the next page. What do these people have in common?

▲ Some Buddhists are famous. The Dalai Lama is the leader of the Buddhists of Tibet. He is famous all over the world

▲ Richard Gere is a famous actor. Many people know that he is also a Buddhist

▲ You can tell that some people are Buddhists by the clothes they wear. Here we can see Buddhist nuns and a monk

▼ Janet Kovach

▼ Jacques Seneque

But most Buddhists are not famous, and they do not wear special clothes. Many different kinds of people are Buddhists, and Buddhists live in different countries.

1 a) In groups, make a list of things which you think a person needs to be happy in this life.
b) Go through your list and write beside each of them what could ruin this happiness (eg being good-looking – growing old and losing your looks).

2 Still in groups, talk about what makes you unhappy (eg being ill). Again, make a list. Then go through your list and put a tick if you think you could avoid this unhappiness. Put a cross if you think you can't do anything to avoid it.

2 A Man Called Siddhartha

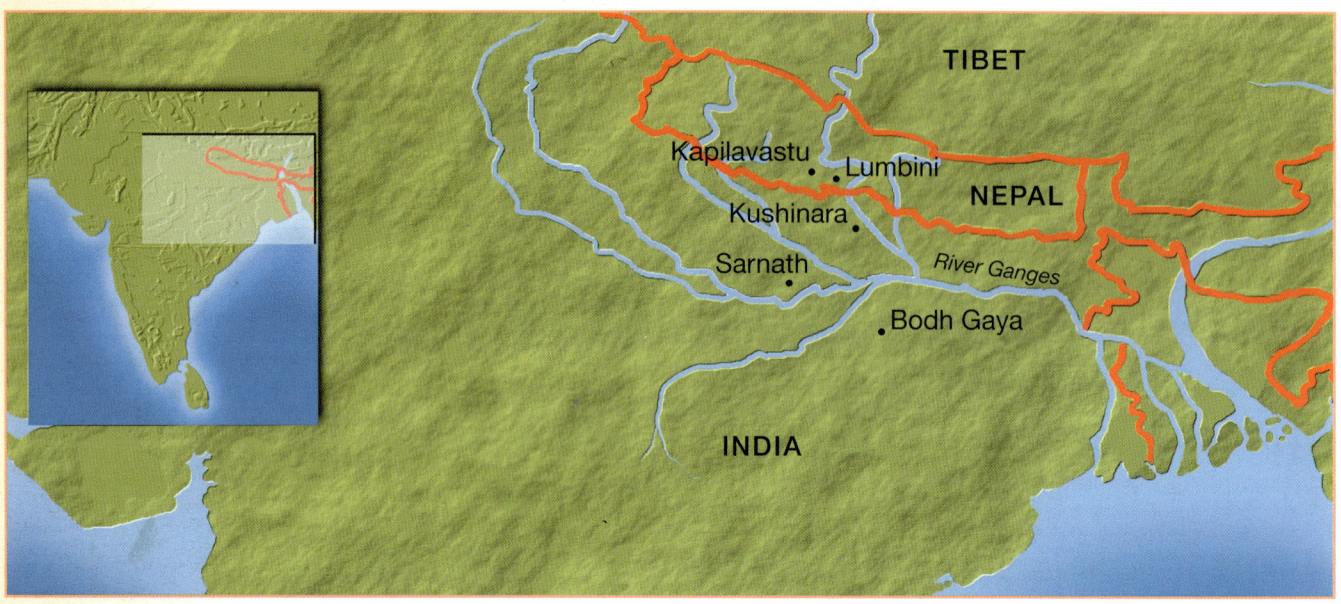

▲ Northern India

TASK

This map shows important places to do with the Buddha. Can you find the following?
- Lumbini – where he was born
- Kapilavastu – where he grew up.

The man who was called the Buddha was born in northern India about 2500 years ago. He was given the name Siddhartha, and his family name was Gautama. So **his full name was Siddhartha Gautama**.

His father was a local ruler, so Siddhartha lived in a palace. He lived a life of luxury. The young prince had servants to do everything for him. He spent his time in sport, music and art. At an early age he married a beautiful princess, and they had a son. What more could he want?

▲ This stone pillar at Lumbini marks the birthplace of the Buddha

There are many stories about the Buddha. They were passed on by word of mouth for about 600 years. Then they were written down.

One story tells how a wise man saw Siddhartha when he was a child. The wise man said that Siddhartha would give up everything for religion. He said that he would become a great religious teacher.

Siddhartha's father didn't want his son to give up everything for religion. He wanted him to take over from him as ruler. So he did everything he could to make his son happy in the palace. He didn't let him hear about anything that might upset or worry him. He gave him everything money could buy.

But in spite of all this, Siddhartha was not really happy. He wanted to find out about life for himself.

▲ What is your dream world? Would you like to be like this? Would it make you happy?

▲ Is this good advice?

1 In pairs, talk about these questions: What do your parents want you to do when you grow up? Do parents always know best?

2 Parents often try to protect their children from things that might upset them. Do you think this is always a good thing? Think of at least TWO examples of:
   a) things you think your parents should share with you;
   b) things they should keep from you.

3 Imagine you are Siddhartha. Write a page in your diary, describing a normal day.

4 If you were Siddhartha, would you want to see life outside the palace, or would you prefer to stay inside and enjoy yourself? Give your reasons.

3 Siddhartha's Quest

▲ *Siddhartha saw four things:*
1. *an old man*
2. *a sick man*
3. *a dead man*
4. *a holy man*

Siddhartha's father had tried to protect him from all the bad things in life. But one day, he went out and saw the 4 things in the picture above. They were to change his life.

They made him realise that he would also grow old and weak and, one day, die. It came as a shock to him. He had never thought about this before. How could he enjoy himself in his palace now that he knew that it would not last for ever? Everything was spoilt for him. Money could not save him from suffering and death.

The last person he saw was a holy man who had given up everything for his religion. Siddhartha made up his mind to do the same. He felt that he needed to take time to think about life and all the suffering it brings.

TASK
- Do you think Siddhartha did the right thing?

Take a class vote on it.
- What would you have done?

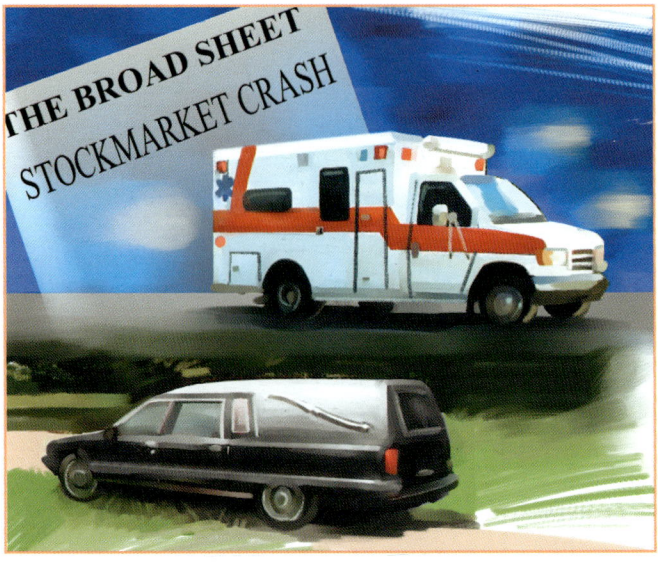

▲ *Some of the suffering that people might see today*

Siddhartha left his family and set out on his search. He was looking for answers to life's questions. It was as if he was searching for a light in the darkness:

> How can there be laughter, when the whole world is burning? When you are in deep darkness, will you not ask for a lamp?
> *Buddhist holy book*

For 6 years Siddhartha lived as a holy man. He met up with 5 other holy men, and learned from religious teachers. He had no money, or house, or fine clothes. He didn't care what he looked like. He ate just enough to stay alive. He grew so thin that you could see his backbone through his stomach. The other holy men admired him.

Siddhartha was near to death when he decided that this was the wrong way to live after all. He had not found the answers to his questions. He still did not understand why we must suffer. He had not found happiness.

So he gave it up. He went down to the river and had a good wash. Then Siddhartha had his first proper meal in years. The other holy men left him!

◀ *A holy man in India today. Siddhartha tried this way of life for 6 years*

1 In FOUR groups, look through a modern newspaper. Cut out pictures or articles which illustrate either old age, sickness, death or holiness (choose a different one in each group). Each group is to make a poster for display.

2 Imagine you are Siddhartha. Imagine how he felt when he left his wife and son. Write an imaginary letter to your wife, telling her why you had to leave.

4 The Enlightened One (Buddha)

▲ *The temptations and enlightenment*

It looked as if Siddhartha was a failure. He had left his wife and child. He had given up the chance to be a ruler. Now had given up the religious life as well.

But Siddhartha hadn't given up his search. He still wanted to know the truth about life. He still wanted to know how to avoid suffering and be really happy. He sat down under a tree and made up his mind that he would not get up until he knew the truth.

As Siddhartha sat there, lots of thoughts and pictures came into his mind. They were temptations. For example, he was tempted by thoughts of sex with beautiful women. Some of the things he saw frightened him. But Siddhartha still did not give in. He sat all night under that tree, fighting with these temptations.

Then, step by step, Siddhartha started to see everything in a new way. And as dawn came, he is said to have become enlightened. In other words, he saw the truth about life.

Enlightenment
The word for enlightenment is 'Bodhi'.
The tree was called the Bodhi-tree.
The place was called Bodh Gaya.
And he was called the Buddha.

Buddhists do not think of the Buddha as a god. They say he was an enlightened person. They believe that he understood the truth about life. The Buddha spent the rest of his life teaching his ideas. He wanted to help others to become enlightened too.

He preached his first sermon in the Deer Park at Sarnath. (Find Sarnath on the map on page 6.) The 5 holy men were there. They were sad when he gave up the religious life. But when they heard him teach, they became his first followers.

What did he see?

There are stories of that night in the Buddhist holy books. But they are very difficult to understand. Remember that this happened 2500 years ago in a foreign country. But it was something like this:

In his mind, the Buddha saw everything that had happened in the past. He saw:

- millions of living things being born, living and dying, and being reborn. He saw life moving and changing like a great wheel.
- that everything was part of one great pattern. Nothing was separate. Everything depended on everything else.
- that people suffered when they didn't want things to change. People suffered because they tried to stop the wheel of life.

Buddhists respect the Buddha as the first person to become enlightened and because he taught others the way. They believe that everyone can be enlightened. Some say that everyone has a 'Buddha nature' inside them, which they need to find.

1. Using page 10, draw a picture-strip for a children's book with FOUR pictures showing the Buddha's Enlightenment. Show:
   - where he sat
   - how he was tempted
   - what he saw
   - what he did.

2. In pairs, talk about these questions: have you ever felt determined to do something, even when other people tried to put you off? Did it take courage to go on? How did it turn out?

◀ *This tree (centre) is said to have been grown from a cutting taken from the tree where Buddha was enlightened. It is at Bodh Gaya. Find this on the map on page 6.*

5 The Buddha's Teaching (Dharma)

The Buddha now started on a life of teaching. Buddhist teaching is called 'Dharma'. This is from the old Indian language of Sanskrit.

Here are some of his most important teachings:

- ## The Three Universal Truths

1 Everything changes

▲ We all change with time. Nothing can stop that

The Buddha taught that:
- everything depends on everything else;
- everything is always changing.

Scientists agree with this. From the smallest atom to the largest galaxy, things are always changing.

2 We all change

The Buddha taught that each person changes too. Nobody stays the same from birth to death. Not only do our bodies change, but also our minds and personalities.

3 We all suffer

Because everything changes and dies, the Buddha taught that life can never fully satisfy us. That is why we suffer. Even if we have everything we want, we know that it won't last! For example, how often do people complain that the holidays are going too quickly, instead of just enjoying them?

▲ What the Buddha meant by suffering – never satisfied

The Four Noble Truths

If you are ill, you want to know:
1. what is the matter with you
2. what is causing the problem
3. how it can be cured
4. what you must do to get better.

The Buddha's teaching is similar. It can be seen as a cure for the world's illness:

1 What is the matter with the world?
The Buddha said that **the problem is suffering** – people are unhappy.

2 What causes the problem?
The Buddha said that **people suffer because they want things** – they always want more happiness, or more money, but it doesn't last.

3 How can it be cured?
The Buddha said that **the answer is to stop wanting things.**

4 What must people do?
The Buddha had been rich, and he had been poor, but he had not been happy. So he taught that **the way to be happy is the Middle Way** – not too rich, not too poor. Then people will be able to be happy with what they have got.

> Buddhism teaches that to be happy, we should enjoy things without wanting them to stay the same, or trying to hold on to them.

▲ *Northern India. The Buddha spent many years teaching here*

Many times, people came to the Buddha with their problems. He listened and asked questions. Then he gave advice that would help them to see life differently. In other words, he acted like a doctor – dealing with the illness of the world.

Key words

Dharma
Sanskrit
Middle Way

1. Think about this on your own:
   do you think it is true that people are not satisfied with life?
   a) Is there something about yourself that you would like to change?
   b) Is there something about your life that you are completely happy with? How long will it last?

2. On page 12 the 'Three Universal Truths' are illustrated with 3 pictures. Working in groups, design, draw and label 4 posters on the 'Four Noble Truths'.

The Noble Eightfold Path

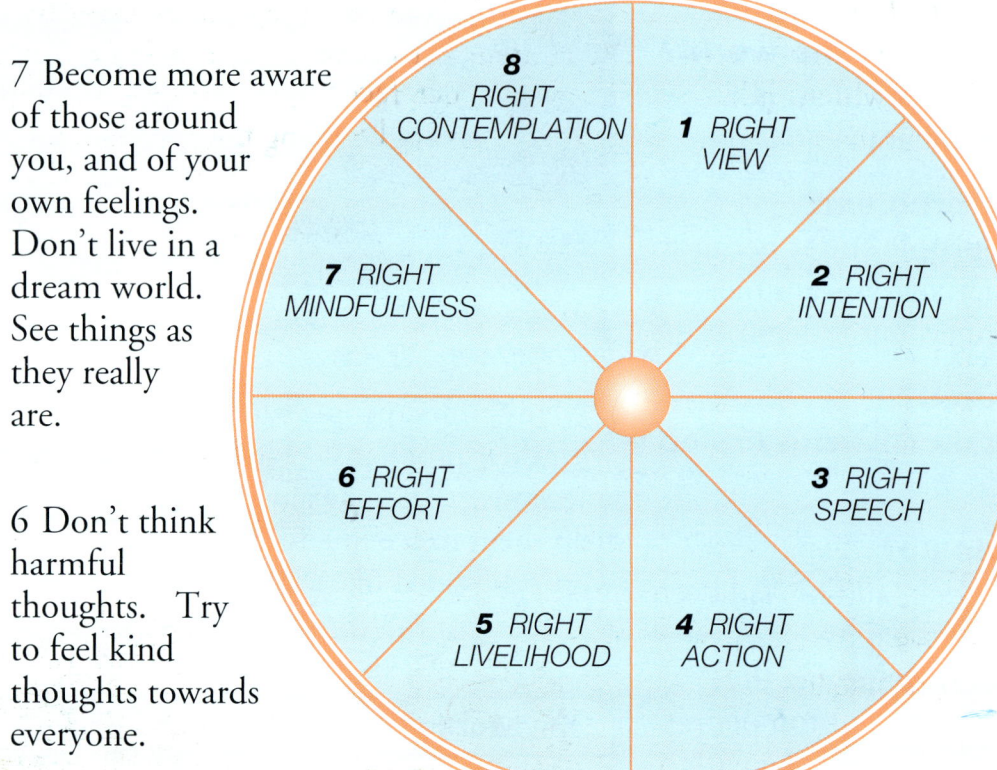

8 By training your mind, you will gradually get rid of hate, greed and ignorance. Then you will be happy and at peace.

1 Before starting on the path, you know that life has suffering and change. You must believe that Buddhism is the answer.

7 Become more aware of those around you, and of your own feelings. Don't live in a dream world. See things as they really are.

2 You need to make up your mind to follow Buddhism.

6 Don't think harmful thoughts. Try to feel kind thoughts towards everyone.

3 Speak the truth, and say things which will help people.

5 Earn your living in line with Buddhist teachings. For example, don't do a job in which you cheat people or take any life.

4 Be kind to all living things (do not kill). Be generous. Be content. Be truthful. Keep your mind clear (do not take drugs).

▲ Buddhists believe they will be happy if they take these 8 steps in life. They call their way of life the 'Eightfold Path'.

- Steps 1 – 2
  People must know what Buddhism offers. They must want to try it.
- Steps 3 – 5
  These are practical things to do, to start living as a Buddhist.
- Steps 6 – 8
  These train the mind to think as a Buddhist.

TASK

Think about the step of 'right livelihood'. Think of at least TWO careers which would be right for a Buddhist, and TWO that would be wrong. (You will need to read what is said in Steps 3, 4 and 5 to think about this.)

How does the 'Noble Eightfold Path' work? Buddhists do not believe in a god who will reward them for following the path. So how do they know it will lead to happiness?

The Buddha taught that everything happens as a result of the conditions in which we live. If you give a plant water and sunshine, it will grow. Without them, it will die. Buddhist teaching is simply advice about the best conditions in which to live.

Buddhists believe that happiness comes from within a person. Some people seem to be naturally happy, even in difficult times. Others are always moaning, even if things are going well for them. So the conditions people need to be happy must be found within themselves. Buddhism can't stop people breaking a leg, or getting old or dying. This is the world we live in. Buddhists claim that they can help people to be content with their life and enjoy it more. They can then face life's difficulties without adding to them by being bitter or hateful.

● **A THREEFOLD PLAN OF ACTION**

How can you spot a Buddhist? There are 3 things which are very important to them:

1 Being good
Buddhists try to be kind to others. They try to follow the Buddhist advice for living.

2 Meditating
Buddhists spend time meditating each day. This is explained in Chapter 11. It helps them to be calm and thoughtful people.

3 Being wise
Buddhists claim to know the truth about life. They believe that everything fits into one big pattern, and that we all depend on each other. They believe that things are always changing, and that we suffer if we want things to stay as they are.

▲ *People can behave so differently. What's the secret?*

1 Take a clean page in your book and write the title 'The Noble Eightfold Path'. Draw a path with 8 signposts on it. Write in each of these the headings for the eightfold path on page 14. As you write down each one, read the book to make sure you know what it means.

Karma

The law of cause and effect

Buddhists believe that everything we do has an effect on us. They call this karma. If you are kind and helpful, you will benefit. If you hurt others, you have to live with the effects. Karma doesn't mean that someone punishes you for what you do wrong. It's a simple fact of life that you will suffer for doing wrong. A Buddhist explains:

> I think of the Law of Karma as simply 'Everything you do has an effect.' If you say a friendly word to someone, that makes you better friends. They may say something kind back. You don't do it for that, but it's the result of your good karma.

▲ We don't always see the long-term effects of what we say or do!

Look at the words in the large box on this page. They are from an early Buddhist book, called the Dhammapada. They say that whatever you think or do today, will make you what you will be in the future. For example:

- A person hates and kills someone. Even if he gets away with it, he will have to live with what he has done. He will carry it around in his mind. It will make him different. It is bad karma.

Of course, people do get chances to change. They can do good things. In time, their good karma may overcome the bad.

> Karma is simply a matter of cause and effect.

What we are today comes from our thoughts of yesterday. Our thoughts today build our life of tomorrow.

If a man speaks with a bad mind, suffering follows him as the wheel of the cart follows the animal that pulls the cart

If a man speaks and acts with a good mind, joy follows him like his own shadow

Dhammapada verses 1, 2

What happens at death?

In India, where the Buddha lived, most people believe in reincarnation. They believe that, after death, a person is reborn into another life on earth. They can be reborn again and again. Their future life depends on the sort of person they have become in this life. The Buddha didn't say much about this. But most Buddhists believe that karma can affect future lives. Exactly how this happens, they do not know.

Beliefs and ceremonies

Do Buddhists have to take part in religious ceremonies to follow the Middle Way?

The Buddha said that, if someone was shot, it was more important to pull out the arrow than to argue about what kind of arrow it was.

In the same way, it was more important for the Buddha to help people to overcome suffering, than to argue about religious ideas about God. Therefore Buddhist teaching does not include belief in God.

The Buddha told his followers not to rely on religious beliefs and ceremonies. They do not work like magic, or like money in a slot.

He also taught that it was more important to do the things he said, than to just talk about beliefs.

This is how the Dhammapada puts it:

> If a man speaks many holy words but does not do them, this thoughtless man cannot enjoy a holy life. He is like a cowherd who just counts the cows of his master.
>
> Whereas, if a man speaks just a few holy words and yet he lives by them ... the life of this man is a life of holiness.
>
> *Dhammapada verses 19, 20*

▲ This photo shows Buddhists making offerings at a shrine. They believe this will have a good effect on their minds. They are NOT asking God for help.

1 Imagine that you are a Buddhist mother or father with a small child of your own. Make up a bedtime story about 'The animals of Ourtown Wood'. The animals live in the wood, but all their actions have effects – on others and on themselves. The story you make up will either show a good deed having a good effect (good karma), or a bad deed having a bad effect (bad karma).

6 The Community (Sangha)

The Buddha travelled around northern India, teaching, for more than 40 years. His followers became known as the Sangha, which means 'community'.

In India at this time, people were divided into castes. It was like a class system. A person was born into the same caste as his or her parents. If you were born into a high caste, you could have an important job. If you were low caste, you had little chance of success. Only the highest caste (priests, called Brahmins) could teach religion and perform religious ceremonies.

The Buddha did not agree with this. He mixed with people from all walks of life. All members of the Sangha were equal. All had the same chance of getting a good job.

The Sangha is important to Buddhists. They don't think you can follow Buddhism on your own:

> You can't do it on your own. You need friends to help and encourage you. That's what the Sangha is for.

Some of the Buddha's followers chose to give up their family life and become monks. Buddhist monks are called bhikkhus. Later, the Buddha let women become nuns. They were called bhikkhunis. It is said that the Buddha's own wife became a bhikkhuni.

The Buddhist monks and nuns travelled around teaching the Dharma. During the very hot, wet months, they met in resting places (called viharas) to study the Dharma together.

As time went by, the viharas became permanent monasteries. Some monks lived there all year round. They agreed on extra rules to help them organise their life together. But they were not priests. There are no priests in Buddhism. All Buddhists are responsible for themselves.

Most Buddhists are NOT monks or nuns. They are ordinary people, trying to live out the Buddha's teaching in their daily lives.

Nowadays, the Sangha is not just monks and nuns, but all those who follow Buddhism and meet together in groups.

When he was 80, the Buddha became ill, and died at Kushinara. His body was burned and his ashes were given to the local rulers in northern India. They built monuments over his remains to remember him. These are called stupas. Many Buddhists visit these stupas.

Key words	
sangha	monastery
bhikkhu	vihara
bhikkhuni	stupa

▲ This picture shows the Buddha on his deathbed

1 Put the title: 'Places in the life of the Buddha'. Look back over pages 6–19 to match up the following:

Lumbini — where he first preached
Kapilavastu — where he died
Bodh Gaya — where he was born
Sarnath — where he was enlightened
Kushinara — where he grew up

7 Different Kinds of Buddhism

◀ Most Buddhists live in the countries on this map

There are now about 350 million Buddhists. Most live in the countries shown on the map, but there are Buddhists living all over the world. There are thousands of Buddhists in Britain.

For the first 200 years, Buddhism spread throughout India. Then it spread to other countries. It changed as it met people with different customs. So there are now several kinds of Buddhists. We shall look at 4 of these in this chapter. All 4 can be found in Britain.

- **There are Buddhists in Sri Lanka, Burma and Thailand.** They worship in the way passed down by the first monks from the time of the Buddha. There are many Buddhist monks in these countries.

- **After about 500 years, Buddhism spread to China, Korea and Japan.** There are fewer monks in these countries. Family life is important.

- **After the 7th century CE, Buddhism reached Tibet and spread to Nepal.** Tibetan Buddhists like to be very colourful.

- **After the beginning of the 20th century, Buddhism came to the West.** Some of these Buddhists are Westernised and modern.

So there are different customs, dress and ways of worship. Buddhists see these as different ways of following the same path to enlightenment.

Monks, Nuns and Lay Buddhists

Most of the people who followed the Buddha led ordinary family lives. They came to him for advice, and tried to follow his teaching. They gave food and money for his work. They were lay Buddhists. That means they had no special religious job.

The Buddha also gathered around him groups of monks (and later, nuns). They had left their families to spend all their time on Buddhism.

Buddhists do not promise to be monks or nuns for life. They can be monks or nuns for a time and then go back to live with their family.

A monk lives a very simple life. He spends his time in meditation, study, teaching and work. He is only allowed to have the following things:
- a simple yellow robe
- a bowl for gifts of food
- a needle and cotton to mend his clothes
- a string of beads to help him concentrate
- a razor for shaving his head
- a bit of cloth - he pours his drinking water through the cloth so that he doesn't get insects in his drink and kill them by mistake.

The bowl is not for begging. The monks do not ask for anything. But they go out each day, and people are glad to give them food.

Ordinary Buddhists put their gifts of food into the monks' bowls. They put their hands together and bow to the monks in respect. They thank the monks for accepting their gifts. It has given them the chance to give to others, as the Buddha taught them to do.

> When asked why he became a monk, Handa, a Japanese monk said:
> I was trying to discover who I really was. I was looking for something I could spend all my life doing.

Most Buddhists are family people. But monks and nuns have played a very important part in the history of Buddhism. They had time to spend in studying the Dharma and teaching it to others. It was mainly through them that Buddha's ideas have been passed on.

Both the lay Buddhists and the monks are important. They are all part of the Sangha, part of the same community. They are there to help each other.

1 Look at the list of things that a Buddhist monk has.
  a) If you could have only SIX things of your own, what would you choose?
  b) Pick the most important THREE and explain your reasons to a partner.
  c) Compare your answers with the rest of the class.

Theravada Buddhism

▲ Monks being given food in London

The kind of Buddhism found in Sri Lanka, Burma and Thailand is called Theravada Buddhism. Theravada means 'the ways of the elders'. It follows teaching handed down by the first Buddhist monks from the time of the Buddha.

Most Theravadin Buddhists would say that the life of a monk is the best way to follow the Buddha's teachings. The monks have nothing else to think about. But not everyone can be a monk or nun.

So family people are glad to support them. In return, the monks teach them about Buddhism.

Most Theravadin monks wear saffron-yellow robes. Early Buddhist monks probably wore this colour because the saffron was cheap. Other Buddhists wear different colours. The colour does not matter. What is important to them is that they live their lives trying to follow the Buddha's teachings.

In Thailand, many young boys spend a short time in a monastery, living as a monk. This gives them a chance to learn more about Buddhism. It reminds them that they belong to the Sangha – the Buddhist community.

At the start of this time as a monk, the young boy has his head shaved. He is given robes and presented to the most important monk of the monastery. After his time at the monastery, the boy goes back home to his family. They often have a party to celebrate.

◀ *Buddhists becoming monks*

The Buddhist temple in Wimbledon looks just like temples in Thailand. The monks there, and some of the people who use this temple, are from south-east Asia. There are also many Westerners who have taken up this form of Buddhism.

▲ *A Buddhist temple in Wimbledon, London*

1 When a young boy spends a few weeks in a monastery, his life changes:
- he cannot play out with his friends;
- he learns lots of new things about Buddhism.

Using this page, work with a partner. Think of 4 more ways his life will change. Decide if these changes are for the better or worse.

Mahayana Buddhism

The Buddhism that spread north to China and then to Japan is called Mahayana Buddhism. The name means 'great vehicle' because it is for everyone, not just for monks.

There are many different forms of Mahayana Buddhism. There are over 100 in Japan. Here are 3 examples:

Pure Land Buddhists

This is based on devotion to a form of the Buddha called Amida Buddha. A statue of Amida Buddha is shown on page 32, where he sits in calm meditation. Its followers keep their mind on Amida Buddha by chanting greetings to him. They believe that he will release them at death into the 'Happy Land'. Its religious leaders marry, eat meat and work at ordinary jobs.

Nipponzan Myohoji

This kind of Mahayana Buddhism is very modern. These Buddhists want peace. Its followers have built peace pagodas all over the world. Handa, one of their monks, explains why:

> By building peace pagodas, we draw attention to the Buddha's teaching that we should not kill. We should respect each other.

▲ The Peace Pagoda in Battersea Park, London. It was built by this movement

▲ A Japanese Buddhist religious leader sits in meditation. Notice how different his robes are from that of the Theravadin monks

Key words

Theravada
Mahayana
Amida Buddha
peace pagoda

Zen Buddhists

Meditation has always been an important part of Buddhism. You will study how Buddhists do meditation on pages 42–45. **In Japan there is a form of Buddhism called Zen. Its followers meditate every day.**

Meditation is a way of training the mind. It helps people become more aware of everything they do in their daily lives.

▲ *A Japanese tea-making ceremony*

To be more aware, they take something ordinary (like making tea or flower-arranging) and become absorbed in every tiny detail. In this way, an ordinary activity can become very beautiful, and a way of calming and training the mind.

▲ *Part of a stone garden in Kyoto, Japan. The small white stones make patterns round the larger stone. The garden helps people to feel peaceful*

Zen Buddhism doesn't think you can get very far along the path to enlightenment just by thinking about it or studying the holy books. They say that sometimes we just know that something is right, without thinking too hard about it. They also say that we need to be aware of everything that is happening in the present moment.

1 a) Working as a whole class, work out and write down, in order, everything that is done to make a cup of tea.
b) Try doing another ordinary activity, like sharpening a pencil, very slowly and carefully. See if you notice things that you don't normally. Share your ideas with the class.

2 Some problems are solved by thinking about them. Other problems are solved by feelings. Which would be better for the following?:
a) doing your maths homework;
b) choosing a colour for your bedroom.
Make a list of FOUR things that need careful thought, and another FOUR which you can solve by feelings. Share your ideas with the class.

Tibetan Buddhism

Tibetan Buddhism is very colourful. The temples have many different Buddha images. There may be large wall-hangings. There are candles and lamps. During worship, words with special meanings are chanted over and over. These are called mantras. At festivals, monks blow long horns, and there may be processions and dancing. People dress up and act out Buddhist stories.

All this is very different from Theravada or Zen Buddhism, where everything is simple. This is because Tibetan Buddhism wants people to use their feelings and imagination as well as their thoughts.

work. They also have other things to remind them of this on-going worship. Prayer-wheels have prayers and mantras written inside them. Small ones, like the one shown below, are whirled round by hand. Larger ones may be set in a wall.

Tibetan Buddhists also write prayers on bits of cloth and hang them up as flags to blow in the wind. So they join with nature in worship.

Study and discussion are important in Tibetan monasteries. The monks check that they have understood the teachings by discussing them with one another.

▲ A Buddhist temple in Tibet, decorated with flags with prayers written on them

▲ Young monks in discussion

Tibetan Buddhists think of worship as something that goes on all the time. They may chant mantras while going about their

Young boys may spend some time in a monastery. It is rather like a boarding school. They are taught by the monks about Buddhism.

◀ Tibetan monks

The most important teachers in Tibetan Buddhism are called lamas. The most famous is the Dalai Lama. He was brought up in Tibet and trained to be their religious leader. But in 1957 the Chinese invaded Tibet. The Dalai Lama escaped to India with many of his followers. He has never been able to go back to Tibet. He still speaks for the Buddhist people of Tibet. Many other Tibetan lamas have travelled to other parts of the world. So Tibetan Buddhism is now more widely known than it was before. Many Western Buddhists follow the Tibetan form of Buddhism.

Buddhist teachers

You can start to learn about Buddhism from books. But most Buddhists say that they need a teacher to guide them.

There are also some teachings which are kept secret. This is because they may be misunderstood. They are only taught to Buddhists when they are ready for them.

Key words

mantra
lama

1 Make a list of TEN things from pages 26–27 that make Tibetan Buddhism so colourful and unusual.

2 When do we hang out flags? How is this different from the Buddhist prayer flags?

3 Talk about which is best: to learn from books or from a teacher? Give your reasons.

4 Find out more about the Dalai Lama. Use your school library and ICT for research.

Buddhism in the West

All the main forms of Buddhism are found in Britain:

1. Some Buddhist places of worship are used by people who have moved to Britan. The Thai Buddhist temple in south London is an example of Theravada Buddhism. The monks and many of the people there are from Thailand. They follow Thai customs. But they do welcome other people to join them.

2. Amaravati is a large monastery in Hertfordshire. It is one of 4 centres set up by the English Sangha Trust. It follows the customs of the forest monasteries in Thailand, but many of its monks are British. People can stay there to spend time in quiet thought and study. They can also visit to share in the worship and festivals, or to hear a talk on Buddhism.

3. Other Western Buddhist groups have been set up to teach a particular Buddhist practice. The Samatha Trust, for example, teaches people something called 'samatha meditation'. This helps to develop inner calm, a strong mind and clear thought. People in the West often live busy lives. They may be worried about work or money. They may not know which way to turn. They can join a class to learn about meditation. The Samatha Trust thinks that this will help them to relax and understand themselves better. It is the first step to seeing what Buddhism has to offer them.

◀ Thai Buddhists in south London

Buddhism and change

The Buddha said that everything changes and that things depend on things around them.

So it is not surprising that Buddhism itself has changed as it spread to different countries.

One Buddhist group in Britain is the FWBO (Friends of the Western Buddhist Order). **It has changed things from the old forms of Buddhism so that they fit into the modern Western world.** This has led some people to question whether members of the FWBO really are Buddhists. But they think of themselves as Buddhists.

FWBO runs centres where people can learn about meditation and Buddhism. People who attend classes are called Friends. Most of its centres are named after the places where they are, for example The London Buddhist Centre and The Manchester Buddhist Centre.

▲ A yoga class run at a Buddhist centre. You do not have to be a Buddhist to go there

Members of the FWBO are not monks. But the FWBO does like people to live in single-sex communities. Some of their married couples have chosen to live apart from each other in this way. This is very different from normal Buddhism where people either live in families or they become monks or nuns.

▲ A Buddhist vegetarian restaurant. Many members of the FWBO give up their jobs and careers to work in businesses like these.

There are many different types of Buddhism. They have different beliefs and practices. Some emphasise one thing and some another. But there are 3 things which are important to all Buddhists:
- the Buddha
- his teachings, and
- the community of his followers.

1 Discuss in class:
   a) Why do you think people find life so stressful, particularly in the big cities?
   b) In what ways is life stressful at your school?
   c) What do you do to be more calm and relaxed?

2 Explain why you would expect the Buddhist restaurant in the photo to be vegetarian. (Look back to page 14 to see what it says about 'right livelihood'.)

8 Going for Refuge

> **TASK**
> A refuge is somewhere you go to feel safe. In a similar way, people sometimes use certain things to get away from the worries of this life. The picture below shows some of the things people take refuge in. Others may find a refuge in friends, or hobbies, or chocolate. In pairs, talk about your own refuges. Where do you find comfort?

Buddhists think it is a bad idea to seek refuge in money, or work, or drugs or another person. All of these things can change and let you down. **Buddhists go for refuge to the Buddha, his teaching (Dharma) and the community of his followers (Sangha).**

Going for refuge in this way is not seen as running away from life and its problems. Buddhists say that it is those people who seek refuge in other things who are running away.

When someone wants to become a Buddhist they say the Refuges and Precepts in front of at least one ordained member of the Buddhist community. The Precepts are 5 guidelines on how to live as a Buddhist. You will study these in Chapter 13. A person repeats 3 times:

> I go to the Buddha for refuge.
> I go to the Dharma for refuge.
> I go to the Sangha for refuge.

People need to know something about Buddhism before they join. But they can't know everything. Going for refuge means that they have chosen to start out on the Buddhist path.

When a person takes the Refuges and Precepts they usually make 3 offerings:

1 A candle
This stands for the light of wisdom, a light to guide them through life.

2 A flower
A beautiful flower will fade and die. This reminds them that everything changes, and all living things will die.

▲ Some things to which people go for refuge

◀ These Buddhists meet in a group to share their understanding of the Buddhist way of life

▲ The 3 offerings of candle, flower and incense can be made at a Buddhist shrine at other times as well

Alan has been a Buddhist for many years. Here he describes why he went for refuge:

> Most things, like hobbies, only affect part of your life. But Buddhism is so big, you can put your whole life into it. You know that everything you do will be worthwhile.

Buddhists hope to benefit by feeling inner peace and happiness. But they don't think this is selfish. They try to be kind to all other living things as well.

3 A stick of incense

Just as the sweet smell spreads out, so will their kindness and goodness spread out into the world. They can make the world a better place.

When people have gone for refuge as a Buddhist, they will try to:
- follow the example of the Buddha
- grow in understanding of the Buddha's teaching
- live out that teaching in their lives
- practise meditation
- help other Buddhists.

1 a) Write out the words that a person says when he or she becomes a Buddhist.
   b) Draw the THREE offerings that the person makes, and write a sentence to explain what each one means for a Buddhist.

2 Talk about why people often like to have ceremonies for important occasions (like joining a religion). What other ceremonies can you think of (these don't have to be religious)?

9 Buddha Images

▲ *A statue of Amida Buddha in Japan*

Buddhists have their favourite images. They often have a number of different images at home. These will stand for the qualities that they most admire and want to develop in themselves.

▲ *This is a modern Western image of the Buddha*

There are many different images of the Buddha. Some try to show what the Buddha may really have been like. But many do not.

Each of the different Buddha images teaches different things about enlightenment. One may teach kindness. Another may teach wisdom. One may teach the importance of calm meditation. Another may teach a Buddhist to put his energy into doing good.

There are male and female Buddha images. Some are kindly and others are fierce. Some are dressed simply and others have royal robes and crowns. Some are brightly coloured or have many arms or heads.

Buddhists spend time meditating on all these different qualities. The different images help them to do this.

> I have 3 Buddha images and some photographs set out on a shelf. I can see them when I meditate. I prefer the simple images showing the Buddha as a real person in history. But I like others as well. Some are very complicated.

▲ *In this image, the sword stands for wisdom. It cuts through ignorance*

Some of the images show rich and beautiful young men and women. These images stand for the inner riches that Buddhism brings, such as happiness.

These images are meant to get you thinking. You shouldn't ask, 'Is this what the Buddha looked like?' or 'Is this image right or wrong?' You should ask, 'What does this image stand for?' or 'What does it tell me about Buddhism?' A Buddhist would also ask, 'What can it teach me about myself?'

We live with images all the time. They are very powerful. They can persuade us to buy one thing rather than another. Here is an example of an image that influences our society:

You won't become more handsome or beautiful simply by buying what is advertised. But it suggests that this is the sort of person who would buy it. If you want to be like them, you should buy it too! We know it isn't really true, but the image works on us all the same.

1 Nobody is the same all the time! We all have different aspects of our personality which come out from time to time – a 'happy me', or a 'sulky me'.
a) Working with a friend, choose the aspect of your friend's personality that you like most. Draw a symbolic picture of your friend to emphasise this aspect of his or her personality. Show this image to your friend and explain it.
b) Choose the aspect of your own personality that you would most like to change. How will you start to do that?

Some Buddha images seem to be full of energy. These are mostly from Tibetan Buddhism.

▲ *This Buddha image shows anger*

A Buddhist explains the angry images of Buddha:

> Anger can be harmful, as when a small child loses its temper and hits out. But the energy in anger can be useful. It can get things done. In these angry images, I see a burst of energy that can overcome difficulties.

Buddhism helps people to look at all sides of themselves. This includes feelings of hate and anger as well as love. Buddhists believe that they should think about their anger. They need to know why they are angry. And they need to learn how to use the energy that is bottled up in that anger. The angry Buddha image is a reminder that they can use that energy for good.

The Buddhist life is sometimes summed up in 2 words: wisdom and kindness. These show that there are 2 sides to Buddhism. One side is to do with learning and understanding. The other side is to do with living in a way that cares for all other living things. In the image of the Buddha below, these 2 sides come together. The image is of a sexual couple. But this image is not about sex. It is meant to show the joining of wisdom (the female) with kindness (the male).

▲ *This image, described above, is called Yab–Yum (mother–father)*

Some Western people may be embarrassed by these sexual images. But they are treated with great respect in Buddhism. Don't forget, they are only images. They don't exist in the real world. They help Buddhists to understand enlightenment.

Some things to look for in a Buddha image

We can learn a lot from the position of the hands on Buddha images. These hand positions are called mudras. Each mudra has a special meaning:

Images of the historical Buddha often have a flame coming out of the top of his head. This shows that he is enlightened. He is also shown with long ear lobes. In India long ago this was a sign that someone was holy and wise.

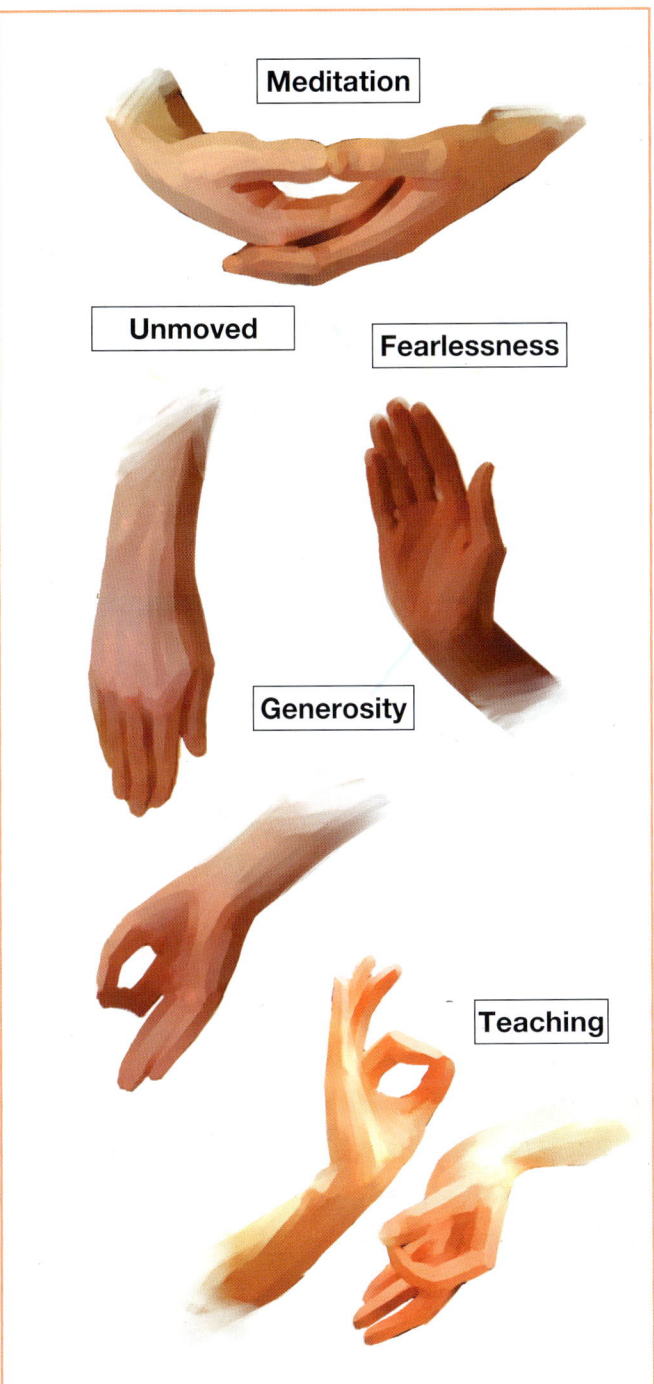

The Buddha can be anyone

If everyone has it in them to become a Buddha (enlightened), then a Buddha image can be anyone. In India, the images are mostly Indian. In China, they are Chinese. Many new Buddha images in the West have Western features. There are also female Buddhas.

1. One Buddha image is an angry Buddha. Read the explanation given. Think of FOUR occasions when it would be right to get angry.

2. Choose TWO of the mudras to copy out and explain their meanings.

▲ These 2 images both show kindness

36

The images on this page are not actually of Buddhas. They are called Bodhisattvas. This describes someone who has put off his or her own enlightenment in order to help others to become enlightened.

These pictures show the Bodhisattva of Compassion (kindness). In China, she is a female. The picture here shows her as a kind, gentle person. In Japan, he is male. The picture above shows him stepping down to help people and with 1000 arms to help people.

▼ This metal object is called a vajra. It means both 'diamond' and 'thunderbolt'. It is a symbol that Buddhism is unbreakable like a diamond, and powerful like a thunderbolt

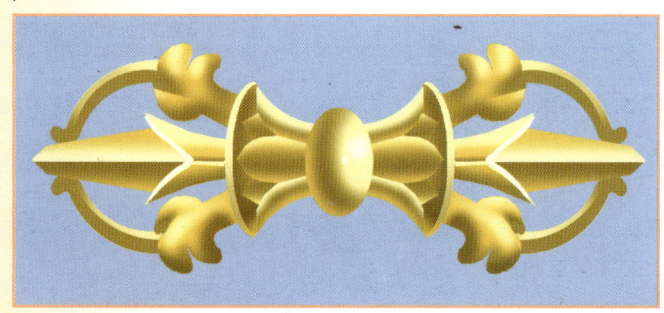

▲ The Chinese version, called Kwan-yin

A lotus flower is like a water lily. Sometimes a Buddha is shown holding or sitting on a lotus flower. The lotus is a symbol of enlightenment. The lotus has its roots in the mud at the bottom of a pond. It grows towards the light. It opens up into a lovely flower on the surface of the water. This is like people's minds. They may start in the mud of anger, greed and ignorance. But they can grow towards enlightenment. They can open up to be loving, kind and wise.

▲ *The Buddha's footprint at Bodh Gaya*

In the first few hundred years after the Buddha's death, there were no Buddha figures. Instead, he was represented in other ways:
- a stupa (a monument built over his ashes)
- an 8-spoked wheel
- a footprint.

▲ *An 8-spoked wheel – for the 'Noble Eightfold Path' (see page 14)*

1 Write out these sentences, putting these FIVE words in their correct places:
Buddha   enlightenment   mudras   images   lotus.
There are many ___ of the ___. They are symbolic. The position of the hands is important. They are called ___. He may be seated on a ___. This is a symbol of ___.

2 The school has decided that it wants an image of the Buddha to stand in the front entrance. It must fit in with the aims of the school. Conduct a questionnaire, asking TEN people at school what qualities they think it ought to show. Find the TWO most popular qualities. Then draw a design to show the sculptor how he or she can include these in the statue.

10 At a Shrine

Buddhist worship is called puja (an Indian word). It is done at a shrine. It may include:
- chanting
- making offerings before a Buddha image
- listening to readings from Buddhist holy books
- speaking short passages together.

Buddhists do not worship the Buddha as a god. It is a way of showing him respect. Buddhists are thankful to the Buddha for his teachings. Worship is also a way of sharing with other Buddhists.

In most places where Buddhists meet you will find a room for worship and meditation. It is their shrine room. It will have a Buddha image. There will be room for people to sit on cushions on the floor. Buddhists may also have a shrine at home.

These things may be found at a shrine:
- Buddha images – there are many different kinds (as you learned in Chapter 9).
- Offering bowls – offerings are made as if the Buddha were there as a guest. On a shrine, there are usually 7 bowls filled with water. They stand for all the things you would offer a guest, like different foods and drink.
- Flowers, candles and incense – to stand for wisdom, death and kindness (these are explained on pages 30 and 31).

There may also be:
- A small bell or gong – to tell people when it is time to start or move on to the next stage of worship.

Key words

puja
shrine
incense

▶ The shrine at the Croydon Buddhist Centre, south London

▲ *A Buddhist offers incense at a shrine*

> Buddhism teaches that we work on 3 levels: body, speech and mind. I think puja is important because it uses all 3. You can put your whole self into it.

Buddhists often chant mantras in worship. These are words in Sanskrit (a very old Indian language). They say them over and over again. Often they do not have a straightforward meaning. They are therefore difficult to translate into English. The sound is as important as their meaning. Buddhists chant these mantras to help themselves on their path to enlightenment.

The most well-known mantra is:

'Om mani padme hum'.

This is what it means:
- **om** – reminds Buddhists of what they want out of life;
- **mani** – means 'treasure' and reminds Buddhists of the Buddha, Dharma and Sangha;
- **padme** – means 'lotus' (see page 37);
- **hum** – reminds Buddhists to be kind and loving.

A Buddhist explains the use of mantras:

> You don't have to know the meaning in a word-for-word sense. You just have to know what the whole mantra stands for.

▲ *Large, beautiful wall-hangings are often used in worship*

1. Describe everything you can see in the photo on page 38 in such a way that someone who has not seen it will be able to imagine what it looks like.

2. Write down any words from a pop-song that don't make sense on their own, but are still part of the song. (This is a bit like mantras.)

Different kinds of temples and shrines

There are many different kinds of places where Buddhists go to meditate, to make offerings or to join in puja.

The simplest of these are stupas. These are monuments built over the Buddha's remains. They are solid, dome-shaped buildings. They may be small or large. Buddhists visit them and walk around them to show respect to the Buddha. Tibetan Buddhists call them 'chortens'. They are highly decorated, as you can see in the photo below. Small shines are built around them where people leave gifts. You can also see a row of prayer-wheels in the photo. (You read about them on page 26).

There are also Buddhist monasteries. They have different names in different countries. Monasteries are often built beside the stupas. The Buddhists who visit the stupas use the monastery's shrines to make offerings.

There are also Buddhist temples. These have rooms for people to gather together. They can meditate or chant there. They can pay their respect to the Buddha by making offerings before a Buddha image. There is no rule about how often a Buddhist should visit a temple. Some go there often. Others go only at festivals or when they feel the need.

▲ A Tibetan chorten

▲ Can you see the monks cleaning this huge image of Buddha in Thailand?

Buddhists sometimes cup their hands together in worship. This stands for a lotus flower (see page 37).

Some Buddhists bow deeply in front of a Buddha image. Some even lie on the ground. They are not bowing to the image, but to the Buddha himself. It is their way of showing that they owe everything they have to the Buddha and his teachings.

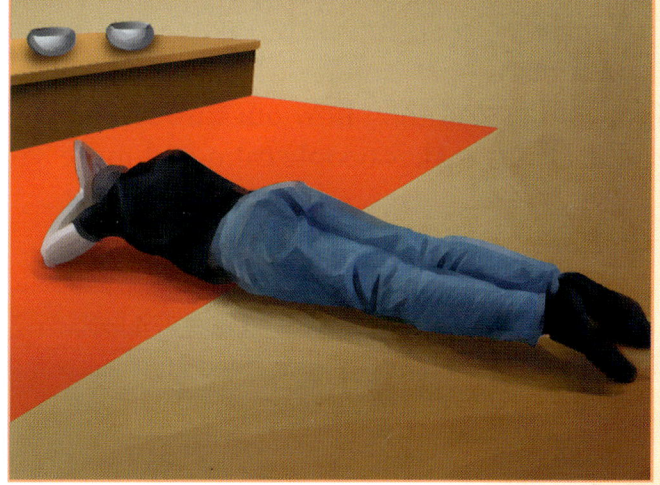

▲ *This image of the Buddha shows him teaching. (You read about the hand positions on page 35.)*

Buddhists may also have small shrines in their homes. This will often be a quiet place where they can meditate.

On entering a shrine room, Buddhists usually face the shrine, put their hands together and bow. Again, this shows that they respect the Buddha.

Key words
stupa
chorten

1. Working with a partner, use pages 40–41 to find SIX different things Buddhists may do at a shrine.

2. Imagine you are a Buddhist. A friend thinks that you worship the Buddha as a god. Write a letter to him, telling him what you do in front of the Buddha image at a shrine, and why you do it.

11 Meditation

> **TASK**
> - Are there any things you become so involved in that you forget the time?
> - Are there other things that you find boring (time passes very slowly and you find it hard to keep your mind on them)?

Meditation helps Buddhists to keep their minds on things. It trains their minds so that they can concentrate fully on every moment. There are 2 kinds of meditation:

● Samatha meditation

This helps the mind to become calm and fixed on a simple object or idea. It trains the mind not to wander.

One way to do this is to become aware of your breathing. You feel the air gently fill your lungs and then flow out through your nose. This makes people calm and more aware of themselves. This is how one Buddhist describes it:

> Sometimes, even just for a moment, it feels as if you are floating at the very centre of the world. All the rush of life around you has stopped.

As people go deeper into meditation, they reach different levels. This is what some people have said it can feel like:
- being filled with joy, like soap powder dissolved in a bowl of water;
- like fresh water bubbling up from a spring at the bottom of a pool;
- like being wrapped in a white cloak.

The best way to judge meditation is by what happens afterwards. If meditation is working well, the person should become calmer and more content. They should be less angry or unreasonable.

▲ A Western Buddhist meditates at a shine in Thailand

▲ *Indian monks make a special pattern (called a mandala) with coloured sand*

If you give your attention to any activity, however simple, your mind will become calm. Look at the monks in the photo. They are making a religious pattern, called a mandala. They are completely involved in what they are doing. This is the important part – not the finished product. When it is finished, it will be thrown away!

Zen Buddhism teaches people to concentrate on ordinary activities, like flower-arranging and tea-making. They also make patterns in a sand garden. These are all chances to calm the mind by concentrating on what you are doing.

1 Here is an exercise to see how still your mind can become.
Breathe in and out. Think about the breath going in and out of your body. Then silently count 'one'. Take another breath, and count '2'. Try to count like this up to 10. If your mind wanders at all, go back to 'one'. Afterwards, talk in pairs about how you felt. Did you find it easy or not?

2 Imagine you are a Tibetan Buddhist. You have just finished making a sand mandala. A non-Buddhist says he thinks you have wasted your time. After all, the pattern is just thrown away. How would you reply? Explain:

a) why you made the mandala
b) why it is thrown away when you have finished with it.

Vipassana meditation

In this kind of meditation, a person takes some Buddhist teaching and holds a picture of it in their minds.

For example, some Buddhists meditate on flowers. They see that they are beautiful now but they will quickly fade and die. This reminds them that all life changes in this way. We can enjoy beautiful things, but we know that they will not last for ever.

Some Buddhists meditate on death. They might imagine a dead body about to be burnt up. We will all die one day. Buddhists believe we should try to keep this in mind. People who have almost died sometimes say that nothing can really worry them again. This meditation is a bit like that. Buddhists say that if you think about your own death, you can be kind to others without worrying about yourself.

▲ *A Zen meditation hall*

Zen Buddhists have halls where they sit to meditate. These are often plain buildings. The monks sit facing a blank wall so that they see nothing to distract them. Another monk walks up and down behind them with a flat wooden rod. He keeps an eye on those who are meditating. If someone gets drowsy, he gives them a hard tap with the rod!

Some Buddhists chant rather than meditate. They chant a mantra over and over. It has the same effect as meditating silently. It helps the monks to concentrate and calm their minds.

None of my little problems seem to matter any more!

People should only try this meditation with the help of a Buddhist teacher. It is a serious matter. It can do more harm than good unless used properly.

Buddhists may meditate on one Buddha image. They remember this image. Sometimes they imagine themselves becoming this image.

For example, they might have a picture in their mind of the Bodhisattva of Compassion (see page 36). They do this to become more kind themselves.

'Right Mindfulness' is the seventh step in the 'Noble Eightfold Path' (see page 14). Buddhists believe that the practice of meditation is one of the best ways to become aware of those around you, and of your feelings.

But meditation is not an end in itself. Meditation should affect the way people live and the way they treat others.

How do you know if meditation is doing you any good? This is what one Buddhist said:
- I don't look for a result after each session. Meditation is a long-term process. It's a regular habit that will gradually help you to change. On the other hand, you hope that each time you meditate you will become a little bit more aware of what's going on around you.

Sometimes, however, people may suddenly see things in a new way.

● Developing Loving-Kindness

Some meditation helps Buddhists to become more kind to others. They think about someone they like, such as a good friend. They think warm, friendly thoughts about them. Then they think of someone they do not like. They think warm, friendly thoughts about them too. As the meditation goes on, these friendly thoughts can spread out to those who live around them. They can spread even further, to everyone in the world.

1 a) Do you think there are some things, like death, that are too terrible to think about?
b) List all the things you have done since you woke up this morning. Talk about what you would have done differently if you knew you were going to die tonight.

2 Copy out what it says about 'Right Mindfulness' from page 14.

12 Festivals

▲ Buddhists in Thailand celebrate the New Year by showing kindness to living things. This woman is putting an eel back into the river

There are no fixed rules about Buddhist festivals. But many Buddhists enjoy celebrating them together. Each festival teaches something important about Buddhism.

1 Wesak – Buddha Day

A most important Buddhist festival is Wesak. This comes at the time of the full moon in May. It celebrates the life of the Buddha. It recalls his birth, enlightenment and death. There may be processions. Shrines may be beautifully decorated. In some places, Buddhists decorate their homes with candles.

2 Songkran Day – New Year

In some countries there is a New Year festival. In Thailand it takes place in April and is called Songkran Day. Water is used at this festival. Water is an important symbol of washing, refreshment and life. So people wash the Buddha images and splash one another with water. They rescue fish from dried-up rivers and put them in fresh water. They also buy caged birds from market stalls and set them free.

▶ These young people in Thailand celebrate the New Year with a water fight

3 New Moons

Almost every month, the day of the new moon is celebrated as a festival in some Buddhist countries. In July, many celebrate the time when Buddha started his teaching.

4 Kathina – Festival of Giving

In the early days, the Buddhist monks used to get together to study during the rainy season. It was too wet to travel around and teach. In many places, monks still get together in the autumn. This is a time when some people like to give them things

▲ These monks in London sit with their offering bowls. The people pass down the row giving something to each

to support them and their work. They are usually given cloth to make new robes.

Tibetan Buddhism is noisy and colourful. They celebrate festivals with dance and drama. They dress up in bright robes. They take part in processions, and blow horns.

Sometimes they make beautiful sculptures out of butter. These gradually melt and lose their beauty. This shows that even the most beautiful things will change and die. They also make beautiful patterns from coloured sand (see page 43). It is the same idea. Buddhism teaches people that they must not cling to things.

▲ This is a colourful butter sculpture

1 Put the title 'Buddhist Festivals'. Draw a picture and write a caption for each of the FOUR festivals on pages 46 and 47.

2 Talk about the festivals that you like to celebrate with other people. Are there any similarities between your festivals and the Buddhist festivals?

13 The Buddhist Way of Life

Buddhism does not set down rules which everyone must obey. There are 2 reasons for this:
1. Buddhists don't believe in a god who sets down laws and who rewards or punishes people.
2. People are all different. What may be wrong for one person could be right for another. It depends on the situation.

But Buddhists believe you have to live with the consequences of what you do.

Instead of rules, Buddhism gives precepts (guidelines). People have to work out for themselves what they mean for their own lives.

● The Five Precepts

All Buddhists try to follow these guidelines:

1 I will not take life

- that means not killing people
- animals too? many Buddhists are vegetarian
- and the Earth! It means not destroying nature

The positive side of this is:
I will try to show loving-kindness towards all creatures.

2 I will not take what is not given

- not stealing
- not trying to get more than my fair share
- not trying to grab at wealth or power or fame at the expense of others

The positive side of this is:
I will try to be generous and willing to share.

3 I will not be greedy

- not hurting other people through sex

The positive side of this is:
I will act responsibly.

The 3rd precept is mainly about sex. But it can be understood more widely. It is about not grabbing at things to satisfy our own desires. So it can be about not eating too much, or about not spending too much time shopping for clothes!

4 I will not say what is not true

- not deliberately lying
- not trying to give the wrong impression
- not even being dishonest with yourself

The positive side of this is:
   I will try to be truthful in everything I say.

5 I will not cloud my mind with alcohol or drugs

- not getting drunk
- not doing anything that clouds your mind and takes you over. This might include things like being hooked on arcade games

The positive side of this is:
   I will try to keep my mind clear. I will try to keep alert and aware of everything around me.

This last precept is very important. Buddhism is all about being aware of the world around you and how you deal with it. People can't do that if they try to escape from reality.

Rules for Monks and Nuns

The 'Five Precepts' are guiding principles for all Buddhists. They are not fixed rules. But they give advice on the best kind of life to lead.

Some Buddhists take on extra rules for a short time. This may be during a festival, for example.

Those who choose to become monks or nuns have many rules. These are needed so that they can live happily together. If these rules are not kept, the monks and nuns may be asked to leave the monastery.

Buddhist monks and nuns live very simple lives. They only have what they need. They do not eat after midday.

1 Write down each precept. Give an example of how following this precept can help others. Give another example of how breaking this precept can cause suffering.

2 Discuss: which do you think is the most important precept? Compare your answer with others.

The precepts are guiding principles. They are not fixed rules. For example, precept 1 says that Buddhists should avoid taking life. This means that Buddhists are vegetarians. They do not want to kill in order to eat. But sometimes they may need to eat meat to keep healthy. In that case, they may eat meat. They must take care of their own lives as well as the lives of others.

The Buddhist holy books say that these precepts are the best way to live:

> He who destroys life, who speaks lies, who takes what is not given to him, who goes with the wife of another, who gets drunk – he digs up the very roots of his life.
> *Dhammapada verse 246*

Buddhists do not expect to succeed all at once:

> Let a wise man get the bad things out of his life ... one after another, little by little, again and again.
> *Dhammapada verse 239*

Buddhists try to develop the 4 qualities shown in this picture. Buddhists say that they are like lights which guide them through life:

Love • Kindness • Happiness • Peace

A Zen Story

There were 2 Buddhist monks named Tanzan and Ekido. One day they were walking along the road. It was very wet and muddy.

As they came round a bend, they saw a beautiful young woman. She stood on one side. She could not cross the mud.

Although he was a monk, Tanzan went up to the girl. He lifted her up and carried her to the other side. Then the monks walked on.

Ekido said nothing for a long time. But when they reached the temple, he burst out:

'We monks should not go near women – especially young and beautiful ones! Why did you pick her up and carry her like that?'

'I left the girl there on the roadside,' Tanzan said. 'Are you still carrying her?'

Right Livelihood

Buddhists who live by the 'Five Precepts' have to think carefully what work they can do. Look at the picture below, for example. Which precept is broken by butchers and soldiers? Business people would have to be honest in the way they treated everyone.

▲ *Here are some of the jobs that a Buddhist would not want to do*

Buddhism and the Environment

Buddhists try to show kindness to all living things. So they try not to damage the earth that they live on. This is how a wise person should live:

> As the bee takes from the flower and flies away without destroying its beauty and smell, so let the wise man treat the world in this life.
>
> *Dhammapada verse 49*

Care for the environment is also a way of following the first 2 precepts:
- It is a way of showing kindness to all living things. It protects their lives (1st precept).
- The second precept says that they should not take what is not given. Buddhists try to take from nature only what is needed. They try not to destroy nature in the process.

▲ *How will you decide what career to follow when you leave school?*

1 a) Draw FOUR lights of any kind. Write in them: love, kindness, happiness, peace. Beneath them write: 'These are like lights to guide a Buddhist through life.'
  b) Write these FOUR things in order of importance. Put the one you think is most important first. Compare your list with a partner, and explain your choices.
2 Choose one of the following jobs: soldier, pop star, vet, car salesman. Which of the 'Five Precepts' would they find easy to keep? Which would they find difficult to keep? Explain your answers.

14 Buddhist Scriptures

▲ These monks in India are reading holy books in Sanskrit. This is the old religious language of India. Many Buddhist writings are in Sanskrit

For several hundred years after the death of the Buddha, teachings were passed down by word of mouth. The earliest Buddhist writings were done on palm leaves, laid on top of each other. They were threaded together and had a board placed on top to keep them flat.

▲ A Buddhist book made from palm leaves

This photo shows that some Buddhists use the same kind of books today. There are also Buddhist writings which are printed and bound like any modern book.

A monkey king loved his people and wanted to save them. They were being attacked and needed to escape. They tried to cross a ravine, using a creeper as a rope, but the creeper was not long enough.

▲ A Jataka Tale: 'the Monkey King'

● The Tripitaka

The earliest holy books were written in Pali, the Buddha's language. They were gathered together about 500 years after his life. They are called the Tripitaka. This means '3 Baskets'. This is because they are collections of writings in 3 parts. This is what they contain:

1 **Rules for monks and nuns.**
2 **Teachings of the Buddha.** The most popular book is the Dhammapada. Some of its verses are used in this book. There are also stories called the Jataka Tales (see above). These are about the former lives of the Buddha. Remember that Buddhists believe we live many lives on earth. Some of the Buddha's lives were as animals, like the Monkey King above. They all show the sort of life you should lead if you want to become enlightened.
3 **Difficult teachings of the Buddha about the meaning of life.**

The king was tall. He held on to the creeper and made himself into a bridge. The other monkeys ran over him and escaped. His back was broken by the strain. He fell and died.

● The Sutras

Mahayana Buddhists have other writings as well. These are written in Sanskrit (see the second photo in this chapter). The most important are the Sutras. This means 'teachings'. They were written long after the Pali holy books. But Mahayana Buddhists believe that they contain the Buddha's teachings.

Like other things about Mahayana Buddhism, these writings are colourful and imaginative. For example, the Buddha is often shown surrounded by thousands of other Buddhas.

Tibetan Buddhists study the Sutras. Then they test themselves by having a debate. One person makes a statement. Then his or her partner tries to find an argument against it. The first person tries to answer. And so on. This is a good way to make sure you really understand something.

But not all Buddhists read and study the holy books. Zen Buddhists do not rely on holy books. They believe their ideas were handed down from one teacher to another, by word of mouth, since the time of the Buddha.

They use riddles called koans. These are short phrases or questions which don't make sense. Here is an example:

What is the sound of one hand clapping?

▲ One Buddhist teacher was asked if a dog had a soul. He replied 'Mu' which means 'No'. But he barked it out like a dog!

These koans stop people thinking in the usual way. They force us to use other parts of our mind. They show that there isn't always a logical answer to everything. Sometimes, for example, we have to rely on our feelings, or common sense. Sometimes we can worry over a problem. We just can't find the solution. Then, when we stop worrying about it, suddenly an answer comes.

1 Put the title 'The Tripitaka'. Draw THREE baskets. Inside them, write what you would find in this collection of Buddhist writings.

2 Make up a tale about a right-living animal: either Daisy the cow or Rover the dog. Use the 'Monkey King' (pages 52–53) and the 'Five Precepts' (pages 48–49) to help you.

15 Women in Buddhism

▲ A member of the FWBO in the West

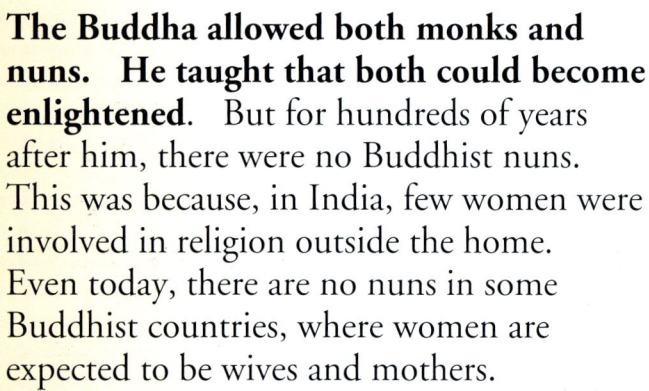

▲ A group of young nuns in Vietnam

The Buddha allowed both monks and nuns. He taught that both could become enlightened. But for hundreds of years after him, there were no Buddhist nuns. This was because, in India, few women were involved in religion outside the home. Even today, there are no nuns in some Buddhist countries, where women are expected to be wives and mothers.

But there is no rule against it and you will find both monks and nuns today in Buddhism. They are treated as equals. In Zen Buddhism, for example, both women and men can become important teachers, called Zen masters.

A nun wears robes like a monk, but they are usually a different colour. For example, some Theravadin nuns wear brown while the monks wear orange. Others have white robes. Both nuns and monks have their heads shaved. This is a sign that they have given up normal life.

Here a nun speaks of her life in the monastery:

> The life of a nun is the same as that of a monk. Jobs are given to whoever can do them. For example, both monks and nuns help with cleaning the monastery and with building work.
>
> All of us have the same chance to grow spiritually. The Buddha made it clear that enlightenment is available to both men and women.

Key words

ordained
reincarnation

In the FWBO, both men and women are ordained as monks and nuns. Most of them are single. They tend to live in single-sex communities and to work with their own sex. They find that it is easier to concentrate on Buddhism that way.

▲ *The Bodhisattva Tara*

Tara is a popular Bodhisattva. She stands for the kindness that Buddhists try to develop in their own lives. She is often shown stepping down from her lotus throne. She is shown ready to help those in need. Tara is said to have lived several lives. In each one she chose to be born as a female. This was to help those people who find it easier to respond to a Buddha who is female.

Buddhism often uses the idea of a mother caring for her children. This shows what loving-kindness means in practice.

Buddhists believe in reincarnation. This means that everyone, human or animal, has lived many lives before this one. According to this belief, it is quite possible that an animal was your mother in a former life.

When Buddhists start to think in this way, it makes them feel more kindly towards all creatures.

1 Read the quotation in the box on page 54. Do you think it is a good idea for monks and nuns to be treated the same?

2 a) Draw a picture of Tara and explain who she is.
b) List the qualities which are often seen as feminine.
c) Do you think men should develop these qualities as well as women?

3 a) Look back at the 'Five Precepts' on pages 48–49. List the qualities that you might need in order to keep these.
b) Do you think it is easier for a man or a woman to be a Buddhist? Explain your answer.

16 The Wheel of Life

The picture opposite shows the Buddhist Wheel of Life. It is like a map. But instead of countries, it has different states of mind. It also shows things that happen in life.

In the centre are 3 animals. They mean:
1 a snake – greed
2 a cockerel – hate
3 a pig – ignorance.
They are biting each other's tails, because greed, hate and ignorance feed on each other.

The middle ring shows 6 worlds. A person moves from one to another:
1 **The world of the gods.** Everyone is happy. Nothing ever seems to go wrong.
2 **The world of aggressive gods.** This is a place for those who would do anything to succeed and beat their rivals.
3 **The animal world**. This is for people who are happy as long as they have enough food, drink, sex and comfort.
4 **Hells – both hot and cold.** Places for those who are depressed or full of hatred.
5 **The world of hungry ghosts**. For those never satisfied. They always want more.
6 **The human world**. Where people are able to study, think and be creative.

On the outer circle is a set of pictures to show how the law of karma works. This is the belief that everything we do has results which affect us (karma is explained on page 16):
- First you are unaware of anything, like the blind man at the top of the wheel;
- Then you start to see things around you;
- But you may try to grab at them, like the monkey after fruit;
- You are carried along by your 5 senses;
- You look for happiness in property;
- And love;
- This only leads to suffering.

And so you live out your life: have fun, work, get married, have children, grow old and die. Only to be reborn again!

Outside the wheel is an image of the god of death. He has a grip on the wheel because everyone will die. But at the top stands the Buddha. Buddhists believe that his teaching can save them from greed, hate and ignorance. It can save them from the endless round of rebirths, as the wheel keeps turning. The picture of the rabbit in the moon is a Buddhist symbol of enlightenment.

TASK

Work in 6 groups. Your teacher will give each group one of the 6 'worlds' above.
- Talk about the sort of people who live in your world. You may be able to name some famous examples.
- Draw a new picture for it. Write a caption to explain your picture.

1 a) Ask one person from each of the 6 groups working on the Task to describe their world.
b) Think about which of these worlds you are living in at the moment.

2 Talk about what it means to say that greed, hate and ignorance feed on each other. Can you think of some situations where this is so? You may like to role-play them.

57

● Re-becoming

The religion in India in the Buddha's day was Hinduism. Hinduism teaches reincarnation or rebirth.

Buddhists also believe in many births. But the Buddha did not believe that each person has a soul to go on from one life to the next. So how can there be rebirth? He believed that the results of our actions can go from one life to the next.

One way to show this is with 2 candles. As the first candle burns down, its flame can be used to light the other. There are now 2 different flames, but the second is the result of the first. In a way, that first flame has gone on in the second.

Buddhism teaches that being born as a human is a rare and precious thing. Imagine a blind turtle swimming in a big ocean. It comes to the surface only once every 100 years. A small gold ring floats on the surface. What are the chances that it will put its head up exactly through the middle of that ring? Buddhism says that we have the same chance of being reborn as a human.

Therefore wasting a human life is bad because it wastes:
- all the former births that led to this rebirth as a human;
- the chance of getting enlightenment in this life;
- all the good that can come from this life.

Tibetan Buddhists believe that it is possible to find the new incarnation of their great teachers after their death. Therefore, when the Dalai Lama dies, they look for a child that is the Dalai Lama reborn. They put the child to all sorts of tests, like seeing if he can pick out the old Dalai Lama's things from a pile of objects. However, this is not the way that most Buddhists think about re-becoming.

The Buddha taught that re-becoming worked in the same way. The actions of one life cause things to happen in other lives. They go on after the first life has ended.

▲ This is a photo from a film in which a young boy is thought to be a reborn lama. The present Dalai Lama was chosen after many tests, but he says it was also partly luck!

● Nirvana

The Wheel of Life shows the world of rebirth. People are driven on by greed, hate and ignorance. By contrast, **nirvana is when the fires of greed, hate and ignorance are put out. Nirvana means 'blowing out'. Then a person is content and at peace**.

Buddhists believe they will only reach nirvana when they finally become enlightened, like the Buddha. But they can know something of the happiness of nirvana by getting rid of greed, hate and ignorance here and now.

> Health is the greatest possession.
> Happiness is the greatest treasure …
> Nirvana is the greatest joy.
> *Dhammapada verse 204*

Some Mahayana Buddhists think that nirvana is another way of looking at this world. Some people are driven by greed, hate and ignorance. Others are freed from these desires and live at peace.

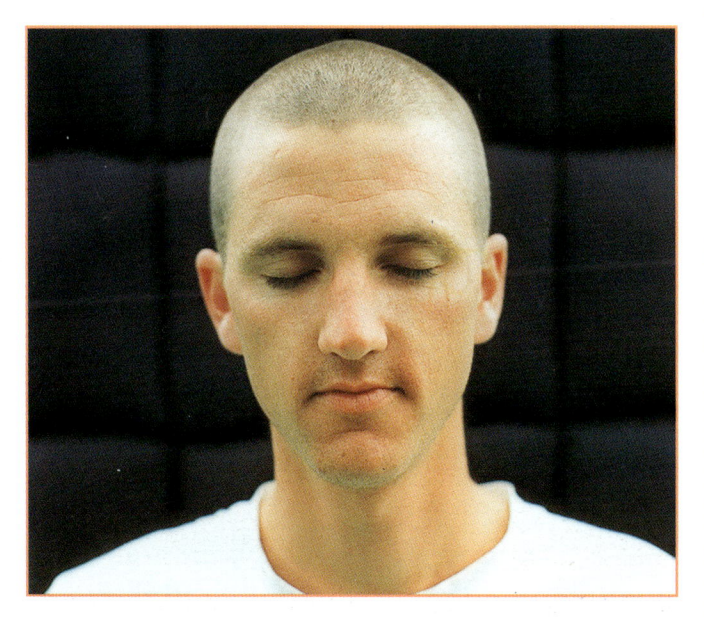

▲ *Buddhists believe they can know something of what nirvana is like*

● Don't ask silly questions!

With ideas like rebirth and nirvana, you might think that Buddhists spend all their time worrying what will become of them. That's not so. In fact, the Buddha said that worrying about such things is a waste of time:

> This is how an unwise person thinks:
> Was I in the past? What was I in the past? How was I in the past?…
> Shall I be in the future? What shall I be in the future? …
> Am I? Am I not? What am I? How am I? Where have I come from? Where will I go?
> *Middle Length Discourse, 2*

The Buddha said that a wise person doesn't worry about all this. He thinks how he can make this present life better for himself and others.

People asked the Buddha many questions which he would not answer. He didn't think it helped to worry about things we cannot know. He taught people how to overcome suffering and find peace and contentment in this life.

1 a) Re-read the story of the turtle and why Buddhists say we should make the most of this life.
   b) How do you intend to make the most of *your* life? What are your ambitions?

2 a) Working with a partner, make a list of FOUR questions that we cannot know the answer to (like 'What happens after death?').
   b) Talk about why people keep on asking these kinds of questions, even when they know there are no answers to them.

17 The Perfections

● The Bodhisattva Vow

Buddhists do not seek enlightenment just for their own benefit. They hope to become kind to all living things.

A bodhisattva is an 'enlightened being' like the Buddha. But they have put off the full experience of enlightenment for the sake of others. They want to remain in this world in order to help others become enlightened.

We have already met Bodhisattvas on page 36. Buddhists may try to become like great Bodhisattvas on that page. To do this, they need to develop the Six Perfections explained here.

▲ *Giving can mean giving money to charity. It also means giving your time and help*

2 Morality

Morality is to do with right and wrong. Buddhists have the precepts to teach them the right way to live.

Can I become like that?

● The Six Perfections

1 Giving

When you give something, you are sharing part of your life with someone else. You may give someone money. You may give them your time, energy and friendship. The more you give people, the more your life is shared with them. In this way, people start to live less selfishly. They become aware that their lives depend on other people.

▲ *Buddhism teaches that wise people are moral. Only foolish people hurt others*

3 Energy

Buddhists shouldn't just sit and think about enlightenment. Meditation is not enough.

They need to get on and do what is right without being afraid.

▲ There are times when we need to act

4 Patience

Buddhism teaches people to be patient. They should not push to get their own way if this will hurt others. They should be kind and patient with other people. Teachers need lots of patience!

▲ There are times when people need to take control, without losing their temper or being unkind

5 Meditation

Buddhists believe that training the mind is very important. This is why they meditate.

▲ How can you make progress, if your mind rushes off in all directions?

6 Wisdom

Buddhists try to understand the nature of life. They try to understand the cause of suffering and how to overcome it. In Buddhism, wisdom is not about reading lots of books. It is about having a clear mind that can see the truth in every situation.

Now I see what it's all about!

▲ Buddhists seek wisdom by thinking about the Buddhist teachings and being honest with themselves

1 Write down the 'Perfections' on SIX cards.
   a) Talk about them with your partner. Put them in order, with the one you think is most important at the top. Write these down, and explain the one you think is most important.
   b) Use the cards again with your partner. This time, put them in order of difficulty. Put the one you think is most difficult at the top. Write down this list also. Explain the one you think is most difficult.

61

18 Living it out

Being a Buddhist can be quite difficult, especially in a non-Buddhist country. The things Buddhists stand for may not fit in with those of the people they live with. Some people might think they are strange because they meditate or are vegetarians.

Those who get ordained as Buddhists are given a new name. This name gives them something to live up to.

We saw Jacques Seneque on page 5. He uses his ordinary name at work. But other Buddhists call him Satyabandhu. This is his Buddhist name. He explains what it means:

> When my teacher gave me my name, he had to explain it, because it is in Sanskrit. 'Satya' means 'truth'. 'Bandhu' means 'friend'. So my name means 'a true friend' and also 'friend of the truth'.
>
> I think I can be a good friend, and I'm interested in the truth.

In thinking about what it means for someone to live as a Buddhist, the following list could be useful. There are Buddhist teachings on all of these things:

- War and peace
- Vegetarianism
- Drink and drugs
- Animals
- Craving for things
- Friendship
- Meditation
- Generosity
- Over-indulgence
- Contentment
- The sort of work you do
- Suffering
- The environment

▲ *This FWBO member wears her scarf only for worship, teaching or meditation. At other times she wears no special clothes*

For further information about Buddhist organisations in Britain, the Buddhist Society, 58 Eccleston Square, London SW1V 1PH publishes the *Buddhist Directory*.

1 a) In pairs, write down at least TWO things that you think might attract someone to Buddhism.

b) Write down at least TWO things which might make it difficult to be a Buddhist in this country.

2 a) Make up a name for yourself. It should say something about you and what you would like to become.

b) Now make up a name for a friend. Explain to them why you chose it.

Glossary

Amida Buddha – the Buddha of kindness

bhikkhu – Buddhist monk
bhikkhuni – Buddhist nun
Bodhisattva – one who seeks to help others to become enlightened
Buddha – the enlightened one
Buddhism – the Buddhist religion
Buddhist – a follower of the Buddha

chant – to sing the same few words over and over on a few notes
chorten – see stupa
compassion – kindness shown to those who suffer

Dharma – the teaching of the Buddha

enlightenment – understanding the truth about life

FWBO – Friends of the Western Buddhist Order, a Western form of Buddhism

image – a statue (of the Buddha)
incense – gum or spice giving sweet smell when burned

karma – actions that have results
koans – riddles used by Zen Buddhists

lama – a Tibetan Buddhist teacher
lay – not ordained
lotus – a flower like a water lily, a symbol in Buddhism

Mahayana – 'Great Vehicle', the form of Buddhism that developed when it spread to China and Japan
mantra – phrase that Buddhists chant
meditation – method of calming and training the mind

Middle Way – way of Buddhism, between the extremes of pleasures and poverty
monastery – place where monks and nuns live
monastic life – the life of monks and nuns
monument – memorial built to a special person or event

nirvana – a state of perfect peace and happiness

ordained – made a member of an 'order' eg a monk or nun
ordination – ceremony at which someone is ordained

peace pagoda – a Buddhist monument to peace
precepts – the 'Five Precepts', the guidelines for a Buddhist lifestyle
puja – worship

Refuges – short statement of commitment to the Buddha, the Dharma and the Sangha.
reincarnation – belief that a person has other lives before and after this one

Sangha – Buddhist community
Sanskrit – very old religious language of India
shrine – holy place, place of worship
spiritual – to do with inner religious development
stupa – memorial to the Buddha, monument built over his remains
symbol – something that stands for something else

Theravada – 'the ways of the elders', the earliest kind of Buddhism, in Sri Lanka, Burma and Thailand

vihara – Buddhist monastery

Wesak – festival for Buddha's birth, enlightenment and death

Index

Amida Buddha 24, 32

Bodh Gaya 10
Bodhi-tree 10, 11
Bodhisattva Vow 60
Bodhisattvas 36
Buddha (the) 4, 6, 10–11, 12–13, 17, 18, 21, 22, 30, 31, 32, 33, 37, 38, 40, 46, 52, 54, 56, 58, 59
Buddha images 26, 32–37, 38, 40

chorten 40

Dalai Lama 5, 27, 58
Dhammapada 16, 17, 50, 51, 52
Dharma 12, 19, 30

Enlightenment 10–11

Five Precepts 48–50
Four Noble Truths 13
Friends of the Western Buddhist Order (FWBO) 29, 62

India 4, 6, 16, 18

Jataka Tales 52–53

karma 16
Kathina 47
Kushinara 19

lotus 37, 41
Lumbini 6

Mahayana Buddhism 24
mandala 43
mantras 26, 39
meditation 4, 42–45
Middle way 13, 17
monks 18–19, 21, 22, 26, 43, 49

mudras 35
Nipponzan Myohoji 24
nirvana 59
Noble Eightfold Path 14–15
nuns 18–19, 21, 22, 49

peace pagodas 24
prayer flags 26
prayer wheels 26
puja 38

refuges and precepts 30–31
reincarnation 16, 55

Samatha meditation 42
Sangha 18, 23, 30
Sanskrit 12, 39, 52
Sarnath 10
shrines 38–40
Siddhartha Gautama 6–11
Six Perfections 60–61
Songkran Day 46
stupas 19, 40
Sutras 53

Tara 55
Theravada Buddhism 22–23
Three Universal Truths 12
Tibetan Buddhism 26
Tripitaka 52

viharas 19
Vipassana meditation 44

Wesak 46
Wheel of Life 11, 56–57

Yab-Yum image 34

Zen Buddhism 25, 43, 44